# Pandemic Pandemonium

## KAREN ROBERTSON

Published by BKR PUBLISHING, 2021.

This is a work of creative nonfiction. Some parts have been fictionalized in varying degrees, for various purposes. The events and conversations in this book have been set down to the best of the author's ability, although some names and details have been changed to protect the privacy of individuals.

---

1. http://www.SayItWithHumor.com

# Table of Contents

# DEDICATION

This book is dedicated to everyone who is sick of hearing about CoVid19, and especially those who have been made sick by CoVid19, lost friends or family to CoVid19, and those who died of CoVid19. God bless us all.

# FORWARD

A FRIEND DARED ME TO write a humorous memoir about CoVid19. I thought it was a silly idea at first, but there was so much negativity being passed around, I decided to take the challenge. I hope you'll be entertained, surprised, and maybe even learn something. Take it lightly . . . I did.

# CORONA VIRUS

CORONA VIRUS IS NOT named after Corona, California. The Coronians should sue for defamation of character.

Corona virus is not named after Corona Beer either, although, all the hubbub about the virus can make you light-headed.

Corona comes from the crown shape of the microscopic virus, but even the queen would agree, they are pretty funky looking crowns.

# AND SO IT BEGAN

ON MARCH 19, 2020, the Centers for Disease Control and Prevention recognized CoVid19 as a vicious killer in the United States, and we, in Southern California, were told to stay at home, isolate ourselves, and watch the reports on TV. I've always been the kind of person that looks at every challenge as a new adventure. I hunkered down with my husband, Barry, and waited to see when they would sound the all-clear bell.

We're used to staying in when temperatures are over one hundred degrees, and sometimes that lasts for weeks. We're senior citizens, so we're free to participate in this challenge without any financial loss. We aren't employed, our kids are grown, and we have three grandkids in college. We receive monthly pension checks, and we have our meals delivered. This pandemic would be a walk-in-the-park for us.

I'd never been told to batten down the hatches and stay home. Well, that's not entirely true. I've had doctors post-surgery tell me to stay home, drink lots of water, and don't lift anything heavier than a glass of milk. This CoVid19 order allowed me to lift whatever I wanted to lift and enjoy my backyard, as long as I didn't sneeze or cough on anyone. At first, I thought the concept was kind of fun. It meant that I was free of all the committees, clubs, positions, and events that attach me to responsibilities.

"Okay, I can do this," I merrily confirmed. I thought, hey, I can kick back and take life easy for a while.

I started every day the same way I have for the past eighteen years since my retirement. Made our bed, got dressed, took an omeprazole (otherwise known as Prilosec), put on make-up, and headed toward the kitchen for a tall cup of coffee.

I tell the doctor I only drink one cup, but truthfully it's about three cups in a huge mug. I brew one pod of caffeine and two pods of decaf. I'm thinking the decaf cancels out the caffeine.

Depending on the weather, I take my devotionals and Bible, cellphone and ear buds to sit in the sunshine on the patio or in my recliner by the fireplace. I listen to Brian Hardin of Daily Audio Bible read the Bible to me as I underline in my own Bible. That is the most consistent thing in my life. God and I meet up each morning to share His Word, pray for friends, family, and our leaders, and run my plans by Him before I get started. The Bible says, "Many plans are in a man's [or woman's] heart, but it is the Lord's purpose that prevails." (Proverbs 19:21)

During the first weeks of the pandemic, we listened every afternoon to the Los Angeles Mayor and our California Governor. Both of them have the most boring, monotone voices and yet can speak for hours. There's nothing worse than listening to bad news from a bad speaker giving us a daily reminder of our bad situation.

I tore the stats page out of the newspaper every day until I could have wall-papered the house with them. After months and months, I threw the pile away. Some day they will be historic and maybe worth a lot of money, but I won't live that long, so I chucked them. I don't mean I expect to die of CoVid19; I just mean it takes fifty years to be considered antique, and I'm already antique at seventy-eight. I won't have another fifty years to find a place to store all those papers.

# STAY AT HOME

WHEN WE WERE TOLD TO sequester in our homes, I thought of some historic events of the past. I remember my mom telling me about the blackouts during WWII, when they had to keep their lights off and cover their windows so if any enemy planes flew over, they wouldn't be able to detect the location of the cities. For the virus, we don't have to cover our windows, just our faces.

In the beginning it wasn't about masks; it was just about staying home for a while. So we settled down and figured it would be over in a few days, maybe a month. Lots of people panicked and went nuts buying toilet paper and paper towels.

If we needed something, our daughter-in-law went to the store and got it for us, and we paid her in toilet paper. I know toilet paper is precious, and I bet everyone who fears running out is trying to cut back from four squares to three as we speak. And I'm not talking about three square meals. I surmise that men can use fewer squares than women, but I won't go into that in detail.

They want me to stay in the house. Okay, I'll stay in the house. I'm a writer, and I can write in the house. But I like people. I like meeting new folks, and my favorite thing to do is interview them. Even strangers walk away from me after a quick chat, wondering what just happened as they've somehow divulged their family history and all their secrets.

I started leaving the gate open in hopes a couple of Jehovah's Witnesses might stray and come knocking. Two kids came to the door, but they only needed directions, and I couldn't convince them to stay and chat for a while. In fact, they looked kind of scared when I started begging.

# NEATEN THE NEST

WHILE THE WORLD STOOD still, I started cleaning out drawers, closets, counters, and cabinets that hadn't been sorted out in thirty years. One of those things I never had time for. Now I had nothing but time. From room to room I went, bagging and boxing anything deemed useless, worn out, or outgrown. I felt like I was gaining control over our world since I couldn't control the world outside.

I was astounded at how many clothes I had that I never wore, so I turned all the hangers around backward, arranged garments by winter and summer, color, and sleeve length. If the piece of clothing got worn, then I turned the hanger around to show I needed to keep it. At the end of the year, my plan was to give away all the ones I hadn't worn. Being an over-achiever, I felt obligated to wear everything once, so I could turn the hanger around and throw nothing away. "Waste not, want not," my mother always said.

It was unbelievable how much "stuff" needed to go. Rusty kitchen tools I inherited from my mother or my first marriage, books I'll never read, pillow cases my great aunt Beulah embroidered for my hope chest when I was a kid, boxes of files from when I was a teacher, success coach, real estate agent, administrator, clown, and standup comic. I boxed up my custom-made clown costume, all my magic tricks, and my first wedding dress from 1962. It was time to let go of the past.

I thought of all the years of education represented by those files and wished I could just stick a zip drive in my head and download it all for young teachers, sales people, administrators, clowns, and comics. What a waste. No telling how many trees I was responsible for destroying in the pages of notes from every class I ever took.

As Hello Fresh delivered our meals in sturdy boxes, I filled the empties with "stuff to go" and stacked them in the garage. None of the thrift stores were open, so the boxes accumulated as a mountain to fall over every time I needed something in the garage.

I cleaned out my sock drawer and discovered fourteen singles without a match. I need to find that website named Match.com. And in another drawer I counted forty-two bras. That's crazy! I only have two boobs, and they only need one bra a day.

My husband can't throw anything away. Even if it's broken, battered, or bent. One day while he was out chasing his golf ball on the course with three other guys, I emptied out his five T-shirt drawers. He used to be a size Medium, but the truth is, he couldn't wiggle into a Medium without help, and he needs to give up that dream. I carefully folded all the Larges and divided them into short sleeves and long sleeves. He's never mentioned it. I boxed up the sixty-two Mediums and hid the boxes. Yes, I said sixty-two! That was in April, and he has never missed them or mentioned their disappearance. I know he knows I did something because I labeled the drawers when I finished. If he doesn't mention missing any of them by next April, those boxes are going to Goodwill.

When I ran out of drawers and cupboards to clean and organize, I moved on to the garage and discovered we have a car, three sets of golf clubs, a tractor, and a riding lawn mower in there.

I couldn't stop myself! I was on a roll and decided we had too much furniture. So I gave away a loveseat and lamp from the living room, a cat house with a climbing pole from the bedroom, a desk and chair from the office, a twin bed from the extra bedroom, and my son's wooden highchair. (He's fifty-four years old.) We pulled out the carpet, put new carpet, gave the old carpet away, and *voila*, it was like having a new house.

Since I didn't feel pressed for time or the demand to get out of bed early, I bought blackout curtains for our bedroom. Now I can sleep all day if I want to, but I have important things to do . . . like get dressed?

There was still one room that was out of control. I helped my grandson Les start a used LEGO sales business when he graduated from high school, and it had expanded to a whole room. His store is named Les Loose Link on the internet at www.BrickLink.com[1].

When he was confined to his home on account of CoVid19, he and his parents drove over and moved EVERYTHING LEGO out of our house. It took them longer than they expected because I was busy kissing their feet! And, yes, there is quite a market for used LEGO sets and pieces.

---

1.    http://www.BrickLink.com

# ENTERTAIN MYSELF

THERE ARE A FEW THINGS I never do. I never watch daytime TV, and I don't do jigsaw puzzles unless I'm away on vacation. I always thought jigsaw puzzles were for people who had nothing else in the world to do.

Desperate times call for desperate measures. I set up a card table in the middle of the living room, started a jigsaw puzzle, and turned on the TV. Multi-tasking has always been a way of life for me, so while I watched TV and worked on a puzzle, I called my maid-of-honor from forty-eight years ago, and we talked for two hours. She lives in Denver, so we probably hadn't talked in a couple of years. Okay, I'm one week down, and I'm soaring.

For the next couple of weeks, I did twelve jigsaw puzzles of various sizes from 150 to 500 pieces. Most of them I could finish in one sitting. When I had finished them all, I put the card table, chair, and puzzles away and said, "What's next?"

I refuse to do a thousand-piece puzzle. I need to finish now and then. I don't like to do a puzzle that holds me captive more than one day. I've got important things to do, but only if they can be done in the confines of my house.

# TOILET PAPER

WHEN THE PANDEMIC WAS first announced, I thought, "Oh, cool, I'm restricted to the house. That means no city council meetings, no chamber of commerce, and no business meetings." Then I got the message, "no toilet paper."

In the past, nobody gave toilet paper a second thought. When we were young and had two kids and worked full time, there were never any extra rolls of TP, and we often made last-minute runs to the store. We never considered it a big deal or had a reserve twelve-pack on the shelf. Now there's only two of us, and we'll be wiping happily for years to come. We always stock up on everything as if it's going to extend our life if we still have toilet paper, paper towels, and napkins left.

Suddenly, toilet paper is as rare as gold, and there is a black market out there selling rolls of it on the streets.

I'm retired, so I look at things differently. No toilet paper? That's no big deal. Kids now days have never experienced a Sears Catalog in a one-holer out behind grandma's house near the barn. I have. No toilet paper doesn't scare me a bit, but I don't know where in the heck I'd find a Sears Catalog these days, and all the magazines are too slick.

No paper towels? Use a cotton towel. No toilet paper? Use a washcloth. They can be used, washed, and used a million times. It's an ugly thought, but I raised my babies with cloth diapers, so those of us older set could manage it.

For the first few months, only my husband went to the store. After six months, I took my first grocery shopping trip. I was more excited than the first time I went zip-lining. I must have walked up and down every row, just to look at the colorful labels.

To my surprise, one person greeted me. "Hey, Karen! How're ya doin'?"

Bewildered, I looked at the masked face and long dark hair, with no clue who it could be.

"Uh, uh, who am I talking to?" I asked, feeling stupid.

"It's me," she said, as she jerked off her mask.

"Oh, hi. Long time no see," I quipped. Still didn't have a clue who she was.

"I'd recognize your voice anywhere," she said and moved on.

Really? Was I talking when she saw me? Maybe I was talking to myself or a box of corn flakes. I haven't had much conversation lately.

# TRESPASSING

MAYBE A MONTH OR TWO into the pandemic, my best friend, Penny, and I determined to have lunch together. I picked out a place halfway between our cities and a place perfect for social distancing. The Mt. San Jacinto Junior College parking lot. Wide open with lots of eucalyptus trees and shade. The college was closed down, so there wasn't a single car in the lot. We each packed our own lunch and a box of "show and tell" stuff to share. We are both creative in different ways, so we always have things to show each other. I packed a couple of rocking camp chairs, and the plan was solid.

We parked on the street because the entrances to the lot were all blocked off, forbidding entry. We grabbed our rocking chairs and boxes and schlepped them into the parking lot under the shade of the trees. The temperature promised to be eighty-two degrees, and we were looking forward to a nice afternoon together.

We set our camp rockers at least six feet apart with the breeze to our backs and settled in. We did a little Bible discussion, broke out our lunches, had plenty of laughs, and shared our artistic efforts.

Two hours into our visit, we were interrupted by a baby-faced security guard in a little golf cart. He was a size or two bigger than his uniform, and he didn't bother getting out of the vehicle he was wedged in.

"You ladies need to vacate the premises. This is government property, and you aren't allowed to be here." Someone gave him a badge and some authority, so he felt the need to shoo off two old ladies in camp chairs who had already been there for two hours in a completely empty parking lot. I guess it took him two hours to get up the nerve to face us two menacing women, or it was the first time he looked up from his Facebook account and discovered us sitting out there in the wide-open parking lot.

Without leaving her chair, Penny said, "We paid our taxes, so technically we own the property." That didn't make him happy, and he became more adamant about running us off.

He repeated the same sentence. "You ladies need to vacate the premises. This is government property, and you aren't allowed to be here." Maybe he'd been practicing that line from the handbook for rent-a-cops.

He must have felt so powerful. I'm surprised he didn't pull his gun, and we could have hollered police brutality like everyone else does. But we're all for law and order, so we packed up our "show and tell" boxes, lunch bags, and chairs and left the parking lot only to set up camp again on the bordering sidewalk by our cars for another two-hour laugh-fest over being run off government property. Fortunately, we did not appear on the front page of the paper the next morning for illegal trespassing.

# TV

THANK GOODNESS FOR old age. Because of CoVid19 there hasn't been a new program on TV for months, so we either watch sixty-year-old programs we watched in our youth, or we watch Antique Road Show and make a guessing game out of what the appraisal will be from when we watched it last time. Or reruns of Pawn Stars or Pickers and try to remember whether they struck a deal or not. Even the Andy Griffith Show and Murder She Wrote were starting to look good to me, but I've seen every Golden Girls, and they are my favorites to this day.

Another favorite is Jeopardy, but we play a modified rendition when our grandson is with us. The contestant on TV chooses the clue, I hit "pause," and my grandson gets the first shot at answering. If he passes or I think he's wrong, I get to answer, and if I pass or my husband thinks we're both wrong (he always thinks I'm wrong), then he gets to try his answer. I hit "play" to hear the correct answer, and whoever was right gets a point. Barry hates it that we make him answer last, but if we didn't, he'd win every time. After all, he crammed four years of college into six years way back in the 60's and has a memory like a steel trap for useless information.

We only watch the TV news for the weather, because everything else is depressing. I'd rather watch a two-hour car chase than the news.

On the 4th of July, we watched the fireworks and enjoyed the patriotic songs on TV, but we missed those chest-vibrating blasts we experience at a live show.

# LAUGHTER

I USED TO BELONG TO the Association for Applied and Therapeutic Humor. It's mostly doctors, nurses, clowns, teachers, counselors, and therapists. They have actually done scientific studies and proven that laughter makes you happier, healthier, live longer, learn faster, be more creative, and have better relationships. Everyone wants those benefits. Here's the kicker. It doesn't make any difference whether the laughter is real or fake. So if you don't have anybody to laugh with, you can just fake your own laugh-fest, and you will get all the same benefits because laughing releases endorphins, no matter what motivates the laughter. Just don't let anyone see you doing it, or they'll think you're nuts.

Learning the value of laughter prompted me to do a TEDx speech on Humor; you can look it up on Karen Robertson TEDx, Livin' Life Laughing.

I had shingles a few years back. What a painful disease! I thought my ribs on one side were broken. When I described the pain, the doctor diagnosed my Shingles without even looking. I picked up some meds, went home, took off my bra, sat in my recliner, watched forty-eight episodes of Golden Girls, and laughed those shingles away in less than two weeks. The laughter was wonderful, and the pain pills were great, too.

The Bible says, "A merry heart does good like a medicine." I say, let your merry heart erupt into laughter, and let it all hang out with joy.

Someone sent me a speech by a doctor talking about CoVid19. He said if you contracted the disease and your lungs became congested, you should get down on the floor on all fours (knees and forearms). Put your face on the floor with your rear-end pointed up and cough, cough, cough to get the congestion to come out of the bottom of your lungs. I know this isn't an attractive position, but it could save your life.

My mom had pneumonia and my doctor advised me to cup my hands and beat on her back where the pneumonia resided and that would break the congestion loose. It worked, so the Downward Dog position seemed logical to me. Fortunately, I haven't had to try it yet.

# WEDDING

WE HAD FRIENDS WHO planned a wedding during CoVid19. Counting the bride and groom, there were to be only ten people and two dogs in attendance. That sounded doable with plans to social distance, wear masks, and stay low key. The bride bought a beautiful dress, and they spent a boatload of money renting a venue and ordering food, flowers, and accessories.

The groom's parents were holed up in a hotel, since their home had just sold and the escrow on their new home was pending. All their things were in storage, so Dad had to order shoes from an online company, and Mom borrowed shoes that were too wide, too long, and too tall. She was afraid she'd fall off them and into the cake, so she practiced walking back and forth across the hotel room, steadying herself on the dresser.

The bride's parents drove from Colorado to San Diego to attend. The rehearsal went well as the parents got acquainted for the first time. They were enjoying dessert when the bride's mother confessed that she just got word from Colorado that her CoVid19 test she took before traveling had positive results. Positively bad! And she was ordered to get home and in quarantine for two weeks. She and her husband piled in their car and headed back to Colorado. The wedding was canceled, the dogs' rented tuxedos had to be returned, and everyone went into quarantine mode again.

The groom's rings weren't ready, the mother-of-the groom is still slopping around in over-sized shoes, Dad's wearing his work boots because his wedding shoes haven't been delivered yet, the bride is beside herself in tears blaming her mother for the mishap, and the dogs really don't give a rip because neither of their tuxedos were of their liking anyway.

# NANOWRIMO

THE PANDEMIC CREATED a perfect time for NaNoWriMo (National Novel Writers' Month). Over 350,000 writers around the world attempt to write a 50,000-word novel in the month of November. They may not be novelists; in fact, they may not even be writers, but someone told them, "Hey, you should write a book," and they fell for it and decided to try . . . at a rapid pace. This challenge is not for sissies. It calls for writing approximately 1667 words per day for 30 days.

The CoVid19 incarceration provided a perfect time for me to give it a try because there wasn't much else I could do, and it didn't cost anything. Believe it or not, it can be physically draining and does have some occupational hazards. I scheduled every day for spiritual, mental, physical, and nutritional health: started the day with my Bible study, then wrote for three hours, walked from one to four miles, made sure I ate three good meals, and slept at least seven hours every night.

I did NaNoWriMo in 2018 and ended up with a pinched nerve in my behind, bursitis in both elbows, and a book to present to an agent after editing it twelve times over two years.

In 2020, I made sure to change sitting positions in different places and different cushioning. I rotated between the recliner, a rocking camp chair (the same one I used to trespass on the college campus), the outdoor swing, the patio chairs, and standing up at the kitchen counter. I finished my novel in twenty-one days, unscathed and feeling good.

During that time, I walked over fifty miles and maintained my same weight. I think the book is better than the last one and won't take a dozen times to edit.

CoVid19 was almost a blessing because if I hadn't been ordered to shelter-in-place, I would have been visiting friends, going to movies, eating out, and letting every distraction tempt me. I am human. But when I was living like a hermit, NaNoWriMo was a great challenge to take up the time. When I was trying to think up 50,000 words, the time flew by unbelievably fast, and I stayed CoVid-free!

Each night writers log into the NaNoWriMo website to update the number of words they've written, and it is graphed with forthcoming statistics and badges won along the way.

The NaNoWriMo district leaders planned Zoom calls for us each week. What do writers do on a Zoom call with a bunch of people they don't know? Writing sprints! The leader starts a timer and says, "Go," and for the next twenty minutes all you hear are fingers flying across the keys to see who could write the most words on their story during those brief minutes. Running sprints leave you breathless. Writing sprints leave your fingers aching and your carpel tunnel throbbing, but you haven't broken a sweat.

There were more than 350,000 people who, when asked, "What did you do during your lock down in the month of November?" can answer, "I WROTE a 50,000-word novel in 30 days" . . . or "I TRIED to write a 50,000-word novel in 30 days" . . . or "I STARTED to write a 50,000-word novel in thirty days but gave up on day #15 when I only had thirty-six words done."

Ten of us from the Diamond Valley Writer's Guild decided to take the challenge together, so every Monday we met for a Zoom call to encourage one another and check our progress. We set our goals and met weekly to encourage each other and talk about all the distractions and victories along the way. We called ourselves the NaNo Challengers.

What a great way to spend a month when CoVid19 is keeping us all at home and forbidding us to plan big Thanksgiving get-togethers.

Half of us were "plotters," carefully outlining our plots and plodding through them, adamantly sticking to the plan. Others were "pantsers," flying by the seat of their pants and letting the characters in the story run rampant through the chapters like a bunch of entitled teenagers.

I finished in twenty-one days, so they all admitted to hating me just a little bit. But some of them have jobs and other obligations. On the last day of November, as a group we had written 363,989 words.

One male writer made his weekly report from a tropical beach, otherwise known as a phony background, selected from the computer program, while another posed in front of an alien space ship and wrote fantasy. The females in the group were more conservative; one posed with a background of books, while another made her appearance in a large tree and whined that following her plot outline had her "up a tree."

Our group of NaNo Challengers was terrific, and we agreed the group encouragement helped us reach our goals. We shared tutorials for Dummies, recipes, laughs, and word count. Our youngest member often zoomed in while making his breakfast at 1:00 pm. Five of us finished the 50,000-word goal, three reached their lesser goals, one has bed sores from sitting too long in the same place, and the last one got lost in her research and ran off with a traveling encyclopedia salesman.

During our meetings we took a home tour of a beautiful cabin in Big Bear, California, where it was snowing as four writers holed up to write. Another time, we got a look at the snow in Big Sky, Montana, when one member had a vacation there.

We all agreed that CoVid19 drove us to take the NaNoWriMo challenge just to redeem 2020 and have something to show for it besides a collection of masks and complaints.

# MASKS

I REMEMBER THE FIRST time I finally "masked up" and ventured out to the grocery store instead of sending my husband for emergency purchases. Some masked man came up to me and laughingly said, "Hey, where's the masquerade party?" I thought that was hilarious at the time. After months and months of it, it wasn't so funny anymore. We all looked like we were going to a masquerade party, but nobody was having fun.

I used to get to the door of the grocery store and realize I forgot my bags. Now I get to the door and realize I forgot my mask. I return to the car to get my mask, and then I get to the door without my bags. Now I'm keeping masks in my bags, so I only have to make one trip back to the car.

Women who wear burqas must just shake their heads at us making such a fuss over wearing masks.

Some masks just look like a wad of gauze while others sport political messages, personal opinions, funny facial features, dopey sayings, and advertisements.

What about those who wear the masks under their noses or under their chins? Isn't that kind of like wearing Depends around your knees? Or what about those who are driving in a closed car by themselves and wearing a mask? Who are they protecting, an imaginary friend?

Barry plays golf, and the courses opened up quicker than some other businesses. I think some wives had something to do with that.

The restrictions were different in every county. When he'd call for a tee time, he'd always ask about the rules.

Does that mean that CoVid19 behaves differently in different counties? In our county, golfers were required to wear masks upon entering the pro shop, but not out on the course. In some counties, golfers are restricted to one person to a cart . . . unless there weren't enough carts; then two was okay? No high fives or back slapping. No picking up someone else's ball. No sharing score cards, so the number of strokes is left up to the honor system. What a concept!

When I look at myself in the mirror with a mask on, I'm afraid when this is over, I'll have ears like a monkey. I wear my hair very short and my lipstick is covered up by the mask, so I have to wear earrings to make sure people know I'm a woman. There are other clues, but men aren't supposed to look there. Of course, nowadays, there are men wearing earrings and women with tattoos, so who knows what lies beneath the mask?

My husband made his mask out of a baseball cap. He cut off the brim and half of the crown, turned it upside down, and snapped it behind his neck. So much for that cap. He didn't want to put anything behind his ears because his hearing aids are back there, and they take precedence.

If he's not playing golf with his firefighter and cop friends, he keeps his sanity by visiting his cowboy friends. They aren't big on hugging or touching anyway. They save that sort of stuff for their horses.

IF YOU CAN GET COVID19 through the mucus in your eyes, what good is a mask if it starts at the nose. Shouldn't we have full face masks? At one point I cut two holes in a brown paper bag, put it over my head, and thought that would be the best protection I could get, but my husband wouldn't let me leave the house. It's okay for him to wear an upside-down ball cap, but I was restricted from wearing a brown paper bag. Go figure.

Our son had his wife make a mask with a loop over the top of his head and one that ties at the back of his neck. When he's working alone in his cubicle, he can just drop the loop from the top of his head down on the front of his neck temporarily. Leave it to a couple of engineers to figure that one out. Who knew masks could come in so many different designs?

Aha, the plastic-covered ones that perch on the forehead and come down over the face to the chin. Now it makes sense, but no matter what I try, my glasses fog up. And if you slobber, that's a mask failure for sure. When I see someone with one of those plastic shields, I think it's my dentist, and I automatically open my mouth.

I can see the advantage to wearing a mask. Especially for those who are mouth-breathers and stand around with their mouths hanging open, the slobberers, and the droolers. The mask saves the usual embarrassment.

I saw a mask designed with see-through plastic in the front for the deaf, so they could read the lips of the speaker. That's a laugh because it wouldn't be for the deaf person; it would be for anyone who talks to a deaf person. So the deaf person comes up to a stranger and hands them a card that says, "I'm deaf, but I can read lips . . . here, please put on this mask so I can see you talk. Never mind that ten other people had to wear that mask today." Stupid!

My friend Robin is a sweetheart. She started making masks one after another as soon as we were required to wear them. Her kids and grandkids ordered more for fellow employees and friends. She lost track after she had made over fifteen hundred.

My daughter-in-law borrowed my sewing machine to make masks for our family. It was old, had lived a good life, and served me well. When she called to tell me it broke, I can't say I was sorry. I was actually thrilled. I'm not buying a new one because then my friend Robin would have me making masks. That's her joy, not mine. I'm a writer . . . did I mention that?

Someone told me the masks look like chin diapers half the time. I think the funniest sights are men who have long beards hanging out from under their masks. It looks like they're eating a squirrel.

Little children who are new to the world will recognize people by their hair, ears, and eyes. Those of us who are older don't usually look strangers right in the eyes, so unless we recognize their walk, their rear end, or their voice, we might walk right by a friend and not even notice them. Children, on the other hand, will have a different perspective.

At my age, hearing is a challenge at best, and now everyone's voice is filtered through a mask. "My moise is mo mumbled I can mardly be merd. Emeryone sounds like they are speeging through mush."

My mask fell off the other day, and I felt like I'd flashed someone. Shocking!

# LOCK DOWN

LOCK DOWN IS A FAMILIAR term to me. I was a school teacher for over thirty years. A couple of times an irate parent showed up with a gun, and we got the "lock down" signal which meant, lock the door and crawl under the desk. I'm not a small person, so when I managed to squeeze myself under a student desk, there were lots of parts of me hanging out. . . front and back. Somehow I felt safe, because I was told that protocol would save us.

It took me back to other years when we were supposedly safe from a nuclear attack or an air raid or something if we marched out on the football field, lay down on our stomachs, put one forearm under the face and one forearm over the back of the head. The forearm under my face was good; it kept grass and ants from going up my nose, and the one on the back of my head kept the birds from crapping in my hair.

A friend my age said she remembers having to don gas masks for some sort of drill, but they may have had a flatulent student that year. I don't remember any gas masks, but I do remember flatulent students.

We had fire drills where we stood up, lined up, and trooped out the door single file, marching out to the playground to burn up in the hot sun in case there was a fire in the building. One time, there actually was a fire in the adjoining open field, so we stood out in formation, breathing the smoke while we waited for the all-clear bell to ring so we could go back in the safety of our air-conditioned classroom.

Unfortunately, the secretary who was supposed to sound the all-clear bell thought the fire alarm was a drill, didn't know there was a real fire, didn't bother to leave the building, and was busy taking a smoke break in the workroom.

Of course, there were earthquake drills for those of us in Southern California. That was another crawl-under-the-desk drill. Later in my career, I worked in an office that had been a storage room with only one door and no windows. A heavy-duty earthquake hit after school hours, and I dove under my big desk (not a student desk, because I had finally been promoted to administration) and huddled there as the whole building shook. I figured, if the roof caved in, so would the desk, and all they'd find would be a flattened female or an angry administrator. I doubted anyone would think to look in that storage room for days.

Shortly after the quake, my office was moved to a tiny upstairs room in a rickety old building. I put a note downstairs on the front window that said, "In case of earthquake, don't forget I'm upstairs."

Now we are at the mercy of our government leaders to keep us informed. They tell us we should be united, and yet in my lifetime, I've never felt so divided by race, creed, values, religious beliefs, political sides, environmental issues, and shopping decisions. People have actually gone to war in the parking lot over a roll of toilet paper. Heaven help us if there is ever a shortage of Q-tips or toothpicks!

# HOLIDAYS

HOLIDAYS WERE THE STRANGEST. Some of them we spent sequestered at home, and some of them we got together with family, but never in a public place and never more than ten people. We flew to Montana for our grandson's graduation from high school. We knew he could only have two tickets, so we were prepared to stage at our daughter's house until after the ceremony. At the last minute, some of his classmates decided they needed to make a political statement by doing something our grandson would not condone, so he didn't go to his graduation and neither did we. But we had a great time with the family celebrating his achievement in their backyard.

Halloween was weird. We live in the country, so we never get trick-or-treaters anyway. We've tried to lure them by hanging a bag of candy on the gate, but that didn't attract anything but ants.

Twenty years ago we started celebrating Halloween with the Great Pumpkin Contest. Eight or ten friends and family who didn't want to be home with the Trick-or-Treaters joined us for dinner.

Barry would buy a giant pumpkin, and I would put a huge chart up on the wall with everyone's name on it. Then, while we carved jack-o-lanterns, each person entered their guesses on the sheet. They guessed the height, weight, and circumference of the giant pumpkin. When they finished guessing the number of seeds and the scoops of goop, we roasted the seeds and gave the big pumpkin to the winner with the most points. We also judged all the jack-o-lanterns, lined them up on the hearth, laid the whole family on the floor, and took a photo of the carvers and the cut-ups.

During the pandemic, I wouldn't think the kids would want to wear masks after wearing them every day for months.

"Dang, Mommy, do I have to wear a mask AGAIN?"

I wanted to say, "What's all the fuss about wearing a mask? I wear a mask every day, and nobody gives me candy."

# HAIRCUTS

MY HUSBAND WEARS HIS hair in a flat top. As the weeks went by without a haircut, his hair just got taller and taller. Desperate times call for desperate measures, and he asked me to see if I could find the clippers and give him a flat top. I did . . . well . . . it was kind of flat . . . if he cocked his head to the left a little.

It's shocking to see women who haven't been able to get their hair dyed for months. I've seen women morph from blonde bombshells to silver foxes to gray ghosts. I'm beginning to look at people and wonder if I'll ever recognize them again.

I have short hair, so I need a haircut every four or five weeks, but months went by, and I was afraid I was going to have a mullet with a ponytail.

# EXPOSED

MY HUSBAND WAS EXPOSED to someone who tested positive for CoVid19 after they spent the day driving in a pickup truck together, so we had to get tested. It took five phone calls to set it up. 1. We called the doctor. 2. The doctor's assistant called us back to get our contact info. (We've gone to that same medical group for forty-nine years; you wouldn't think they'd have to ask.) 3. Another caller set up the appointment. 4. Someone called to confirm our birthdays (They haven't ever changed.). Are you kidding me? 5. Another person called to tell us how to go through the test area. Our appointment was at 8:00 am on Monday morning. We arrived ten minutes early, rolled down both windows, a nurse on each side shoved Q-tips up our noses, and we were off.

When a friend heard we'd been tested, he said, "I couldn't take the kind of test that goes up your nose to your brain." I'm not sure he'd have to worry. They wouldn't find anything in their ultimate destination anyway. He had to go to urgent care and have his mouth swabbed.

I didn't have that kind. Mine just seemed like they doodled around in my nose hairs. It takes all kinds.

# CURFEW

WHEN I HEARD THERE was going to be a curfew from 10:00 pm to 4:00 am, I laughed out loud. I'm never out after 10:00, and neither are any other elderly people who are in danger of CoVid19. Does CoVid19 only go out at night? Is the danger worse during those hours? What insane person thought that one up?

The people in the greatest danger are the elderly. They don't go out after 3:00 in the afternoon because the traffic is too heavy. Why in the world would I be out after 10:00 pm? Unless my defibrillator went on the fritz, and I'd be headed to the hospital. Is that allowed? I don't actually have a defibrillator, but I did go to the Emergency Room once about midnight with high blood pressure. I guess that would be forbidden.

WHENEVER I HEAR THE word "curfew," I am reminded of my mother's favorite story about the curfew she and Dad imposed on me when I was about sixteen. I'd been coming home late several times in a row, and my parents weren't a bit happy about it.

Another teenage couple asked my boyfriend and me to go to the drive-in movies in a neighboring town. My folks said I could go, but I had to be home by midnight. The drive-in showed three films on weekend nights and they went past midnight, so I said we'd leave after the second movie.

When the second movie was over, it was about 11:10, and I suggested we head for home. The driver said, "Oh, let's just watch a little of the third movie and then we'll go." They watched a little, and then they watched a little more as I pouted in the backseat, begging to go home so I wouldn't get in trouble.

At one o'clock we arrived in front of my house. The driver was laughing at me because I was almost in tears I was so mad. He said, "I'm glad I'm not the one who's going in that house."

At that moment, I reached over the seat on my exit, grabbed the keys out of the ignition, and said, "You are ALL going into the house and explain to my parents why I wasn't home on time."

My mother loves to tell how I paraded my boyfriend and the other two kids into my parents' tiny bedroom to stand at the end of their bed and explain how they kept me from being home on time. Thank goodness my dad didn't throw off the covers and accost them, as he slept in the nude, and that would have made the night even more memorable.

Curfews are for kids, just like Trix are for kids. People my age are sleeping from 10:00 pm to 4:00 am, interrupted only by trips to the bathroom. Our drive-in movie days ended over half a century ago.

# ZOOM

HOW DIFFERENT DOES my calendar look? It used to be full of meetings, doctor appointments, and lunch dates. Now it reminds me that I drive a Mazda. Their old tagline used to be Zoom, Zoom, Zoom.

Zoom has been my favorite new toy. It gave me the outlet I needed. Ahh! People . . . at last. I opened my first Zoom meeting on April 15. If I can figure it out, anyone can figure it out. You can Zoom from anywhere to anywhere as long as you have WIFI.

For the first couple of weeks Zoom let me stay connected for an unlimited amount of time. After a few meetings, they started warning me that they were going to pull the plug at forty minutes. When they were sure I was hooked, they started kicking me off at forty minutes. So, I bit the bullet and paid the $14.95/month so I could become the Zoom Queen.

The first Zoom I planned was a surprise 75th birthday party for my husband. He's a cowboy, and most of the family showed up in cowboy hats and toothpicks in their mouths (that's my husband's trademark since he quit chewing tobacco). I made him a one-cup birthday cake with one candle, and we sang happy birthday from three states. He was definitely surprised because he'd never seen a bunch of friends and relatives on the computer screen before. But in some cases, that's a good place to keep them.

I'VE BEEN LEADING A Bible study in my home for many years, and most of the women are over eighty. I call them my Bible Babes. When I suggested we could meet by Zoom, it was completely foreign to them. I planned a training session, and we spent a good thirty minutes just helping each woman get logged in. Some had a little coaching over the phone, but six of the nine attend by Zoom, one comes in by cellphone, one walks to my house and shares my screen, and one has a defective tablet. That's pretty good for a bunch of old Bible broads.

OUR DAUGHTER AND HER family live in Montana, and we're lucky if we get to go there twice a year. Our son and his family live just a mile from us, and we see them at least once a week for dinner. With Zoom, we lasso our Montana family and bring them together with our California family for a visit, something that is quite rare in person. What could be better than having our kids and grandkids all in one place . . . virtually? Nothing! We don't have to make meals or do dishes or pick up the tab.

Our extended family, even though they are spread around the country, stay close through regular reunions. Every three years, we have a wild reunion complete with a talent show, Olympics, card games, and a variety of other events from golf to ziplining. There were eighty-three of us at the last reunion. On Zoom, there is nothing like a family reunion, where you can mute anyone who misbehaves or send private chats about what Aunt Tilly is wearing or Uncle Jed's half-chewed cigar. You just have to be careful you don't accidentally send a private chat to the wrong person about Mary Jane's latest tattoo of a rhinoceros on her forehead she swears her psychiatrist recommended, for her mental health.

The cool part is these folks live in Canada, Missouri, Montana, Arizona, Washington, and California, and in the click of a computer button, we can all be together. If the conversation gets too boring, I can check my email on my phone, cut my toenails, or start a game. We've had scavenger hunts and word games, which usually result in a generous amount of trash talk, put-downs, and a lot of laughs.

If kids can't trick-or-treat on Halloween, and nobody comes to the door for candy, what in the world do you do? I realized we weren't going to have our usual Giant Pumpkin contest, and Barry and I would be home alone. I quickly put out a Zoom invitation to the whole family for an impromptu costume party. Twelve hearty souls attended with crazy costumes. I didn't even recognize my sister who came as a snaggle-toothed witch with green skin. She said she started her make-up process at 2:00 in the afternoon and finished by 3:00 and sat around looking like a witch and unable to eat in fear of messing up her makeup until our call at 6:00. If there had been a prize, she would have won. Our family doesn't care about prizes, they'll compete wholeheartedly for bragging rights.

WITH THANKSGIVING ON the horizon, I was feeling a little sad. My parents passed away a long time ago, and with CoVid19 restrictions, it didn't seem prudent or obedient to the directives given by the governor to invite a bunch of people to dinner. I quickly put together an impromptu Zoom get-together with the extended family to talk about everyone's plans for Thanksgiving. Three generations showed up from three states, thirty-one family members who decided to make it into a dog show. I lost track of the number of canine family members who got their turn on camera, but it was great fun.

THANKSGIVING WAS NICE with only six of us here: my son Jason, his wife, Cecillia, their son Les, Cecillia's Mom, Barry and me. We played Cornhole in the backyard during the afternoon, and when we were all pooped out, we ate for the rest of the day. I bought a turkey breast and a smoked ham from Costco. My daughter-in-law bought mashed potatoes already mashed and a salad to throw together from Costco, and her mother brought homemade sweet potatoes (I think she worked the hardest). Thank you, Costco.

I'M THINKING I COULD save a boatload of money on Christmas cards this year by just Zooming whatever I was intending to write on cards. No buying cards, searching for new addresses, writing letters, purchasing stamps, and licking envelopes. I can save my tongue for talking with my peeps on Zoom.

I SIGNED UP FOR AN art class on Zoom and found there were probably four generations of students from a five-year-old to me. The five-year-old produced a work of art, and then there was me. When it came time to share my work, I turned off the video and pretended like I didn't know how to turn it back on.

MY DAUGHTER-IN-LAW let me know about a Belly Dancing Class on Zoom. Forty years ago I took belly dancing classes when my belly wasn't as qualified, but now that my belly is more than qualified, I signed up. What could be better than learning to belly dance in the privacy of your own bedroom?

I didn't have a costume, so I put on my black bra and low-cut tights. When I entered the Zoom, I entered without video—I thought. I couldn't see me, but evidently everyone else could. . . so my daughter-in-law informed me later. Oh, well, it was only women . . . I think. I did make sure to shut the blinds and even pulled the blackout curtains. Nobody should see this belly in action.

WHEN WE COULDN'T GO to the gym, I discovered Silver Sneakers on the computer. They offer all kinds of classes for senior citizens: Yoga, Pilates, chair workouts, five-minute warm-ups, dance sessions, and balance classes. I took one of each and quit. Variety is the spice of life, but repetition is monotonous.

MY HUSBAND AND I INVESTED in Creator Films. They make family-friendly movies with a Christian flavor. Once a month we have an investors' meeting on Zoom, and we get to converse with other investors and the producer. We've invested in three local start-up banks, and they all went belly up, so I'm holding out the belief that God can do better than that.

FINANCIAL PLANNING can be done by Zoom. In fact, it is less intimidating. When you hear what the IRS is going to do to your gross income, you can hide your tears.

THIS WAS THE YEAR WE should have been celebrating my 60th high school class reunion, but it was cancelled because of CoVid19. The planning committee probably gave a sigh of relief, but I decided to Zoom the get-together. There were 100 kids in our graduating class from Livingston High School in the Great San Joaquin Valley of California. Thirty percent of them have passed away, and about fifty-five percent of them either don't know how to work a computer or they don't give a damn anymore because only twelve alumni showed up, and we had a great visit for two hours. The next day we did it again, and nine of us visited for another two hours. I guess three of them had enough after the first day.

One of the girls I'd known since third grade, and she still looked the same, or my eyesight isn't as good anymore. I swear, my Japanese and Filipino friends never age, but we pale faces sure do. I even put on my heavy make-up, did my hair, wore jewelry, and dressed up . . . from neck to waist. Halfway through the two hours, I got a Charlie Horse in my calf and had to dance around the room to get it out. I'm sure they saw I still had on my pajama bottoms.

I HEARD OF A FUNERAL on Zoom. Now there's the ticket. No looking for something to wear that speaks of bright spring, sunshine, and gaiety, or too dark and dreary so you look like the one who died. No worries about tears that cause your make-up to run because you can wipe your nose on your sleeve and call it good. The trick is to leave the video turned off so all they see is your profile photo with the kids and the dog.

"Celebration of life" is a term often used in place of funeral. How do you celebrate on Zoom? Get up and dance around the room after the service? If you attended in person, there may be tears, and I hear a person with CoVid19 might carry the virus in their tears, so stay clear of anyone crying, cutting onions, or laughing too hard.

Memorials are great. I had a cousin who waited seven months before he had a memorial for his wife who passed away. By then the hardest part of mourning is past, and people can zero in on some sweet memories of a special person, which was my cousin's case. In some cases, it gives people time to forget all the devilish deeds of a scoundrel and make him out to be a hero. What does this have to do about CoVid19? I have no idea.

BARRY HAD AN APPOINTMENT with his cardiologist by Zoom. The doctor asked if his heart was still beating, and since I was sitting right next to him, I vouched for him. I thought maybe he'd have Barry do some jumping jacks or blow up a balloon, but the doctor is Indian, and we have no idea what he's saying most of the time. We nod our heads and smile. I think he's cute.

# FACEBOOK LIVE

FACEBOOK LIVE IS ANOTHER way to communicate. Our church uses that platform to keep in touch. One of the various pastors will show up with an inspirational message almost daily. There are prayer meetings, baptisms, communion, regular worship services, and interviews. I love them all. We don't have to dress up or drive anywhere. I can cook dinner and sing worship songs, but it's harder when you're eating dinner. Amazing Grace sung with spinach hanging out of your mouth seems sacrilegious. But we can eat dinner and listen to the sermon right at the table.

During the service, we see comments from others who are attending. It reminds us we are together in this, and we encourage and pray for one another. We can also see that there are people all over the world online with us. Wouldn't Jesus have loved to have this mode of connection when he walked from town to town to heal people and tell them about the Kingdom of Heaven? Advancements in technology have opened doors around the world. CoVid19 just gave us time and inspiration to connect in new ways. I've seen and visited with my family, both close and extended, more than I ever have in my life.

RHONDA COREY IS A FRIEND of mine from my career in standup comedy. She lives in Rhode Island, which isn't a hotbed of comedy by any means. She started the Rhonda Corey Comedy Live Facebook variety show called Talk is Cheap. It's genius. Twice a week she has a couple of comedy guests and one serious guest who might be a massage therapist, nutritionist, coach, or a hearing aid salesman.

She interviews them all, and there are lots of laughs because comics think they're supposed to be funny all the time. I'm not. Only if I'm getting paid.

Between the ages of sixty-five and seventy-five, I was a standup comic and belonged to the Christian Comedy Association. I pretty much retired at seventy-five, but when the pandemic hit, every comic in America had nothing but a Google calendar full of cancellations. They were just as retired as I was. What does a comic do when there's no place to perform and no audience to laugh? My friends in the CCA, when they could see no end in sight, got creative. Rhonda was the leader, and I say that because she had the wisdom to invite me to be on her 54$^{th}$ episode. Okay, so she used up most of the good comics while I waited in line.

Rhonda and her tech guy, Alex, put on quite a show. Alex is never seen on camera, but Chewy the dog makes cameo appearances through the "Chewy-cam" where he is zonked out on Quiet Moments doggy drugs.

You can't watch her show without getting involved and having fun. During the second half of the program, she plays a game with the contestants . . . I mean, the guests, and it is usually hilarious. The audience has the opportunity to chime in with their answers and add to the laughs. Rhonda often loses complete control of her guests and has to cut to the Chewy Cam while she gathers herself.

Other comedians from our association of clean comics like Nazareth, Maurice Brown, Marty Simpson, and others have developed comedy shows as well. One comic put on a show for his wife, kids, and the pets, and another did a show at a drive-in theater. I can't imagine telling jokes on a large screen and hearing no laughter while people laugh in their cars, and the crickets are all the comic hears. Correction, people who liked the joke honk their horns

Rik Roberts, past president of the association, busies himself teaching comedy classes and inspiring other comics on School of Laughs.

When people say to me, "Oh, you're a comic. Make me laugh," I hold out my hand and say, "Pay me." They always laugh. It's a nervous laugh, but I've done my job.

If you need to kill time for an hour, go to Youtube and watch Maurice Brown interview me on the Maurice Brown Show. You'll learn the trials and tribulations of a standup comic.

# VIDEO CHAT

ANOTHER DISCOVERY DURING CoVid19 is video chat through Messenger. My grandson taught me how to do it since I have an Android and not an IPhone.

I put on my make-up and comb my hair before calling, but the person on the other end may not have been as prepared, and it can be shocking. Especially when salons and beauty parlors have been closed for months.

In June 2019 our daughter Jodi had a massive stroke and was in a coma on life support for two weeks. After four months of all sorts of therapy, she returned home. She lives in Montana with her husband and her kids, but we live in California. When the pandemic called for all of us to quarantine, her only connection outside the home was for her various therapies several times a week. But when her speech continued to improve, she wanted to video chat because spelling and texting were still a challenge. Video chatting works perfectly. She can hear more words being spoken when her husband is at work and kids at college. Also, I can see her speaking and smiling, and when she gets stuck on a word, I can see her struggling to find the word, and I don't mistakenly think she's gone to sleep or fallen off the chair.

I can stay in close contact with my grandkids, who are all in college, and see their faces. It makes Gammie happy to see where her money's going.

# HOBBIES &
# PASTIMES

NOW IS A GREAT TIME to have a hobby. I've heard some people say they had a hard time spending time on their hobbies because they couldn't buy the equipment or the materials they needed. If making toilet paper snowflakes was your hobby, you'd be in trouble.

Some hobbies involve being around groups of people like shopping, going to the movies, or dancing in a conga line. My husband's hobbies are all outside away from people: golf, rounding up cattle, or welding horseshoes into pumpkins, turkeys, and Christmas trees. He is so creative. Since he was a horseshoer for practically his whole life, he's got a pile of used horseshoes that will keep him busy 'til the cows come home.

Cows don't wear masks, but who wants to kiss a cow anyway? Let's not add Mad Cow disease to the mix. Haven't we got enough problems with CoVid19? Oh, my goodness, I just heard of an ape in the zoo who tested positive!

My hobby is writing, of course. A good cheap hobby . . . as long as your computer is paid for, your WIFI is paid for, and your printer is full of ink.

Normally, I write and have lunch with my friends. Since lunch is out in most eating establishments, I write, and on some days, I live dangerously and don't wear a bra. When we are quarantined and under strict regulations, that kind of freedom is exhilarating.

I used to do oil and acrylic painting, and I thought I might take that up again, but so far, I've painted a turkey made out of horseshoes, some nicks in the paint here and there around the house, and the garage door trim. That wasn't the kind of painting I had in mind.

Normally, I'd be public speaking, leading tours of Historic Downtown Murrieta, California, and taking some comedy gigs. Every dollar I make on my hobbies goes to Rady Children's Hospital to our group called BRICK, which stands for Brain Research in Cancer Kids. Our family started it when our grandson Les was treated for brain cancer at Rady Children's Hospital in San Diego when he was four years old. The name BRICK came from his love of LEGO **bricks**.

Thanks to friends and family, we raised enough money to have a plaque with our BRICK logo placed on one of the exam rooms at the hospital. You can read more about it at www.BRICK-BrainResearchInCancerKids.org[1].

---

1.	http://www.BRICK-BrainResearchInCancerKids.org

# NEIGHBORS

EARLY IN THE PANDEMIC, I found a grocery bag with four bananas hanging on our gate. A couple who live in our neighborhood left them for us. They bought more than they could eat and wanted to bless us. They're in their 90's, so I guess the bananas were too green, and they didn't think they'd live long enough to eat the whole bunch.

We have fruit trees, and thankfully the pandemic didn't keep them from producing. Apples, plums, apricots, pears, and peaches. Barry and I make pies every July, and this year we made six kinds: apple, plum, apricot, pear, peach, and pumpkin. I made one cherry pie, but the fruit came out of a can, so we didn't count it. The pumpkin pies were made out of the Giant Fairytale Pumpkin Barry bought for Halloween.

One summer we made fifty-nine pies. We bake them and stick them in the freezer. During CoVid19, it was a good time to bless all the neighbors with various portions of pie. It made me think of the nursery rhyme . . . Simple Simon met a pie man going to the fair.

Sharin' Karen took her pies,

And to the neighbors went.

"Could you bring some more?" they asked.

"We ate the ones you sent."

# GAMES WE PLAYED

WE ADDED A NEW FORM of entertainment during this pandemic. Cornhole. There are two slanted boards about twenty-seven feet apart. Each board has a hole which is where players hope their bean bags will land and score three points. If the bean bag only lands and stays on the board but doesn't go through the hole, it counts for one point. It's a great game because young or old can play, and you can move the boards closer according to the ability of the players. I saw the boards at a Farmer's Market booth and ordered two of them with my husband's alma mater insignia on them, University of Arizona, a surprise for his birthday. The craftsman who made them called to tell me they were finished, and I could pick them up at the market the following week.

As Barry and I strolled through the market the next week, he espied the two boards with U. of A. on them, and as I expected, he went right to them and tried to purchase the Cornhole boards. The artisan and I had cooked up a prank, and he told my husband they were already sold (the truth). Barry wanted to know why the boards were still there if they were sold. The guy said the people were going to pick them up. (Truth)

Barry said, "If the buyers don't come, can I buy them?"

"No," the man replied. "They'll be here soon." He winked at me.

"Well, could you make another set for me?" Barry asked.

"No," the man replied. "These were really tricky, and I don't think I'll do another set like this."

I thought my husband was going to cry. "How much would you charge me to make another set?" Barry begged. The craftsman hesitated.

I pulled the check I had already written out of my pocket and said, "If I wrote a check to Rick James [the craftsman] for $225, would that work?" and I handed the check to him.

He looked it over carefully and said, "Yes, that will be perfect."

Barry was flabbergasted. He couldn't figure out what just happened.

"Happy late birthday," I said.

After a lot of flustering and blustering, he said, "You got me this time."

Our son made us a scoreboard because we couldn't remember our points from one turn to the next. We learned in a hurry, you don't leave the bags out overnight on the lawn and let the sprinkler soak them. There are seeds inside, and they expand. We did it once, and I'm expecting buckwheat to grow out of the bags any time now.

We didn't want to stop playing after dark, so I bought lights for the boards, and when it's dead dark outside and all you can see is the outline of the board and the hole shining brightly, seems like it is much easier to score. But when we miss the board, we have to crawl around in the dark trying to find the missing bags in the grass.

BOCCE BALL IS ANOTHER good game we started playing. Our grassy areas leave something to be desired. We don't have highly manicured lawns like some city folks, so the ball often gets stuck in a squirrel hole, a gopher hole, or bumps into the root of a tree. All those things just make the game more challenging. I usually can't remember which color ball is mine anyway.

BANANAGRAMS IS A GREAT word game to keep your brain tuned up. Barry and I started playing after dinner each night. We are both the "first child" in our families, so we are painfully competitive, and I keep a running score. I may not be so good at Jeopardy, but words are my game. We've played well over 100 games, and I'm humbled to tell you, I'm still a couple of games ahead.

LUMOSITY IS AN OLD person's video game designed to keep my mind sharp, fingers fast, and frustration level up. If I don't want to leave my computer, Lumosity provides all sorts of timed games to test my mental abilities and keep me on my toes. It is as close as I'll ever come to video games. There are animated snippets designed to drive old people crazy. I emailed them to let my subscription lapse next billing cycle while I catch my breath. They kindly wrote back and said when I resubscribe, they will still have my scoring history. Hmm! Will I really WANT my scoring history?

I HESITATE TO MENTION it, but most recently we've been playing a board game by the uncouth name of Smart Ass. I know, I know, it's a little risqué, but the game is a fun question-and-answer game where you can actually learn stuff you didn't know. You can also be deemed a *dumb ass* at times and have to skip a turn. But it's all in fun and the word "hole" never comes into play.

# NOVEL

THE CORONA VIRUS IS also called a "novel" virus. It's novel because it's new stuff that is being discovered for the first time. I wrote a novel, and it was new stuff. Hmm, who knew? The next novel I write, I hope it spreads like a virus and ends up going viral. Teehee! You've got to admit, that's pretty clever, eh?

# MAKE-UP & JEWELRY

FOR A WHILE I THOUGHT I'd just go without make-up, but my husband didn't see it that way. We had a service person come to the house to give us an estimate on replacing some screens. Barry took me aside and said, "Go put on some makeup; you look spooky." Ya gotta love him. Now, I'm not taking any chances. I put on make-up, dress up, wear earrings, and do my hair before I come out of the bedroom. Heaven help us if the plumber comes and catches me on casual Friday! At least it isn't so shocking when I walk by a mirror.

It became apparent that wearing lipstick was senseless when wearing a mask. My cousin said, "I put on my lipstick and my mask, but by the time I get home from shopping, I look like Tammy Fay Baker." Now that's funny.

# WALKING,
# RUNNING, BIKING
# OR GYM?

GETTING OUTSIDE FOR exercise became very important to me. I have to be honest and say running is not my thing, and I have a million excuses. Maybe not a million, but many. My body isn't built for it. Let's just say my top half is well-endowed, and sports bras are not an option. If that's not enough, I permanently partially tore my hamstring when I hyperextended my leg getting up on water skis when I was fifty-five. I blame it on the guy driving the boat because he didn't pop me up. He thought going slow with the old gal would be a positive thing, but he was just dragging me. I had skied many times, so I know it wasn't my lack of skill. Ha!

Between the ages of sixty-six and seventy-one I did five mini-triathlons called Reverse Sprints. They consisted of a five-mile run (which I walk-jogged), seventeen-miles cycling, and 150 yards in a pool. Ten days before I turned seventy-one, I did the last one and placed second in my age group . . . or last, depending on how you look at it, since there were only two of us

It was after that I realized that I'm not even safe walking. I went with a group to Xtapa, Mexico to a spa resort for a week. On the first day, I joined the walking group at 7:00am and off we went. We were walking downhill quickly on a roughly paved road when I said to the gentleman beside me, "The bad thing about going downhill so fast is knowing that later we will have to trudge back up this same hill."

Apparently, when there is a hole in the road, instead of filling the hole, they put a paver about two inches thick, of the same color, over the hole. The man next to me said, "I try to always look down so I'm not aware of whether I'm going downhill or uphill so it all appears the same to me."

Evidently I was looking up, because my foot hit the paver and I went face first into the pavement. For a moment I couldn't breathe or speak, as I gasped for air. My glasses had a gouge out of them, and to this day, every time I blink or shut my eye I can feel the damaged nerve that runs from my cheek bone up across my eye.

A man in a car was there for me within minutes, and I was shuttled back to the resort where a doctor was summoned and arrived quickly. He examined me and said, "You are so lucky." I never rely on luck. I believe God spared me. The whole right side of my face turned black and every day I visited the doctor and he just said, "You are so lucky." The worst part was spending a week at a spa to get all the pampering treatments, and I couldn't even have a facial.

A few month later, I was walking in my neighborhood on the gravel road, stepped on a large rock and went down like a sack of potatoes. I got up quickly and hoped none of the neighbors saw me.

Less than a month later, I planned to drop off a gift at a friend's house and didn't see a step-down in the sidewalk. Right on my nose again. I rolled over in the grass, looked up in the beautiful blue sky, and thanked God that He was the only one who saw me and again had spared me from broken bones or a concussion.

It's only been a month since I slipped on the ice as I walked across an intersection in Big Sky, Montana, fell flat on my back and bruised my toosh and my pride. So, you see, walking is enough for me.

Walking has kept me sane—or less insane, as it were. There are lots of ways walking can be entertaining, although my husband deems it "boring." Walking with a girlfriend is the best. It saves money on visits to a counselor. Even if the advice stinks, you get to vent for a while.

Walking alone is a good time to meditate, pray, sing, reflect, or catch up on phone calls. I live in the country on the corner of a busy road. One direction I walk along a nice path with the exhaust and noise of traffic and pass other walkers, but I also know if I fall down, someone will eventually find me and call 911. If I walk the other way, the roads are dirt, and it is completely quiet and free of traffic. After being quietly sequestered in the house for months, sometimes I'm just as happy being out among the roaring cars, motorcycles, trucks, bicycles, and people . . . even if we wear masks and just wave at each other.

There's a beautiful lake I like to walk around. Some people wear masks, and some people don't. I got to thinking, if someone runs by me, panting away and I can smell their aftershave, soap, or body odor, doesn't that mean that those molecules are floating into my nose as they run by? If that's true, even social distancing might fail when aided by a breeze.

In some of the later months when the gyms opened, I went to my gym. I wore my mask, took my temperature at the door, slopped hand sanitizer on my hands, and went to work. The signs asked that equipment be wiped down with disinfectant before and after use, which I did. All except the exercise ball. How do you wipe down a huge rubber ball? I didn't know where to start or where to end.

Recently, a neighbor thought perhaps I'd like to learn to ride an electric bike. What fun! She rode hers and I rode her husband's. It was much heavier than the racing bikes I had ridden in the triathlons, and I fell in the driveway before I even got started . . . twice.

Down the driveway we went and around and around the neighborhood. I thought I had it licked but wanted to do one more lap before quitting. At the intersection I met with a dilemma, should I wait for oncoming traffic or turn right. I was getting the go-ahead signal from the man in the oncoming pickup truck, but I turned too wide and ended up in the gravel shoulder of the road. I must have hit the gear that shot me forward, and I couldn't guide the bike back up on the pavement. With my friend, the pickup driver, and the neighbors in their yard looking on, I smashed into their pilaster made of cement blocks with a paver on top.

Bleeding was minimal and again God spared me. The guy in the pickup jumped out and came running to me. "THAT WAS AMAZING," he screamed and gave me a huge high five. Then he added, "Are you okay?" Typical male.

Shaken but laughing, I replied, "Did you get it on camera?"

I walked the bike back to my friend's house, because the chain was off and I was too shaken to ride. I'm sure you would agree by now, I need to stick to walking and keep my head down.

# SWING

MY FAVORITE PLACE IN the world is out in my swing under the spreading sycamore tree. No mask required. I see people walking along the path, beautiful Sycamore trees, fluffy white clouds, green grass, and nickering horses. I hear traffic roaring, birds chirping, the sound of a farrier hammering on his anvil, and the motor on the neighbor's swimming pool filter. I can feel the breeze, and the swing takes me to and fro. I smell the familiar aroma of horse poop and urine, and I know I'm home.

Sitting out there, I've seen two lizards courting, which is pretty funny with the male ducking his head up and down trying to woo her closer. I won't go into details. I saw a hawk swoop down and come up with nothing but bunny fur as the rabbit sped away under the barn. I saw a bird land on the corral fence and try to strike up a conversation with the horse. And toward evening the crows come in by the thousands, and with memories of Alfred Hitchcock's "The Birds," it's time for me to go in the house. My husband was in awe of them until he discovered they crapped all over the hood of his beloved pick-up truck.

# GERMAPHOBES

THE PANDEMIC HAS REALLY given the germaphobes a time to rise. I've held to the belief that the reason I've always been so healthy is because I ate dirt as a kid and wasn't very clean until I went to college.

I was raised in a little tiny two-bedroom house about eight hundred square feet. We had one bathroom for the four of us: Mom, Dad, my little sister, and me. The bathtub didn't even have a shower. I remember one time my dad was in the tub with a washcloth over his privates, I was sitting with my feet in the sink pinching pimples in the mirror, Mom was on the toilet, and my little sister was probably just hanging around being a pest.

Mom washed our hair in the kitchen sink every couple of weeks, and we probably bathed once a week, maybe Saturday night so we'd be clean for Church on Sunday morning. I remember sitting in class and rubbing dirt balls off the back of my arms. The first time I had access to a shower was in college, when I lived in a boarding house with sixteen girls. You had to take a number to get a turn at the bathroom. That was around the time the movie *Psycho* came out, so taking a shower was new to me and terrifying at the same time.

Nowadays, a wayward germ couldn't find a home on me if it tried, as I'm sanitized from head to toe. Hand sanitizer is scary. It is so strong smelling, it makes me lightheaded. I take probiotics to nurture some decent bacteria inside my body. Heaven help the germ that comes my way . . . inside or out.

# VOTING, ELECTION
# 2020

THE ELECTION OF 2020 was the weirdest I've ever experienced. I voted, but then I was afraid to mail my vote when there were news stories about truckloads of mail-in votes being dumped. I heard of people actually driving their votes forty miles to the county seat. Wouldn't we all love to know how many legitimate votes got counted?

Enough said about that.

# HELLO FRESH

BEFORE THE PANDEMIC, we started ordering food from a local place. The meals came already cooked in plastic containers. Two minutes in the microwave and *voila*, your meal was ready. After a few weeks of opening plastic boxes of everything from pancakes to chicken dinners, they all started tasting the same.

In March we switched to Hello Fresh delivered meals. We graduated from plastic containers to brown bags, each containing all the makings of a fresh gourmet meal. Sometimes I had the stove, the microwave, and the oven all going at the same time. Stop the presses! When I tried to read the recipes, prep all the vegetables, juggle all the cooking tools, while my husband browned hamburger for his twenty-year-old cat who was fed on the floor between me and the sink, it got a little hairy and I was frazzled. The resulting food is delicious, even when I inadvertently leave out a step or two.

The cat died, and Barry finds it more entertaining to watch the CoVid19 count on TV than to wander in and get in my cooking space. He must be tired of getting chewed out. As a result, I stay sane, cooking is so much more peaceful, and the meals are wonderful.

The reason we only order three meals a week is because Barry is a hunter, so we have a freezer full of wild game: venison, elk, buffalo, geese, and ducks. We seldom buy meat from the store. Someone said, "How lucky you are! Meat is so expensive." Ha! They obviously don't know how much it costs to take out-of-state hunting trips.

# SOCIAL DISTANCING

SOCIAL DISTANCING SEEMS like anti-social distancing to me. I don't dare shake hands with anyone. And it really bugs me when someone sticks out their elbow. Who knows where that elbow has been?

My mother used to say, "Never stick anything in your ear smaller than your elbow with a towel wrapped around it." In other words, don't stick anything in your ear. What if someone has been trying to stick their elbow in their ear? Some people are rebellious like that.

This six-foot social distancing is crazy. What good is a six-foot span when they say a sneeze goes ten feet and can fill a room? Stay upwind and hold your breath when you pass by someone. Pull your shirt over your head and talk out the armhole.

When we had our CoVid19 test, they told us to stay sixty feet apart when you are outside. Yes, they said SIXTY FEET. That goes back to what I said about smelling other people's aftershave or deodorant or body odor. It is still in the air.

Southern California restaurants put up tents so they could serve outside. Why does eating outside lessen your chance of contracting CoVid19? Should I eat out in the backyard? When they put the tables in a tent, doesn't outside dining become inside dining again?

# TO-DO LISTS

WHEN I WAS IN COLLEGE, I rented a studio apartment from an old man and his wife. I thought they were old then. I was nineteen, and the woman was fifty-one. His name was Tommy, and hers was Wilmuth. She had never worked and didn't even have a social security number yet.

I'd had my Social Security number since I was fourteen. It's easy for me to remember because I took a job in a packing shed, where you were required to be sixteen AND have a Social Security card. I was only fourteen, but the lady at the desk offered to fill out the papers to get my card, so I had to tell her I was sixteen. When I was in my twenties, I wrote to Uncle Sam and told him there had been a mistake I needed to correct, and I got a new Social Security number.

I digress. One day while Wilmuth fixed us coffee, I peeked at her TO-DO list on the table. It said, "Soak feet and file fingernails." I couldn't believe it. I was under so much stress being a married student and going to college full time, I couldn't imagine her kind of life. Now here I am with a TO-DO list that says, Read Bible, Write, soak feet, and file fingernails.

# OUT IN PUBLIC

I'M NERVOUS WHEN THE dentist or eye doctor is breathing in my mouth or eyes. The dentist has always masked-up, so I'm protected from him, but is he protected from me? I don't think peeking under my mask to get to my teeth is going to work. The eye doctor only has that little black paddle he holds over one of my eyes. If I sneeze, he only has that little black paddle to defend himself and swat the spew away.

I WAITED AN HOUR OUTSIDE the guitar store the other day for my turn to enter. They were only allowing two people at a time to come in. All I wanted to do was ask them if they rented instruments. I should have taken my ukulele along to entertain myself and those in line. Or Not!

TSA SECURITY IN THE airport require masks, but when you get up to their counter, they ask you to take it off. Momentarily you are de-masked so they can see if you match your photo ID. I hold my breath and smile.

A FEW YEARS AGO, I canceled my accounts at a bank because they put up plastic shields in front of the tellers. They were bulletproof, but it was just too impersonal for me. Now there are shields at every bank, post office, grocery store, school desks, and nail salon, but they're only plastic. It has become the strangest world.

How in the world does a bank teller distinguish between a masked thief and the masked customer? We all look like masked bandits except for those who wear upside down baseball caps or brown paper bags with eye holes. A teller can't be sure who the bad guy is until he pulls out a gun and says, "Hand over all your cash." The guard at the door doesn't have a gun or a taser. What's he going to do . . . hit them with the door mat?

I've got some history with banks. My dad was employed by Bank of America for over forty years. I thought he was Mr. Bank of America. Everywhere he went, he stuck out his hand and said loudly "Hank Brassfield, Bank of America." I was five years old before I realized our last name wasn't Bank of America. And I was probably seven before I discovered my dad didn't own the bank. I would have figure it out sooner or later because he wasn't allowed to bring home samples.

With this pandemic, I get paranoid about touching things . . . other people, products on the shelves, shopping carts. When I was two years old, my Dad had some work to do at the bank one night, so my Mom and I went along. I skipped around the bank entertaining myself and ended my dance with both hands slapped up against the vault, setting off the alarm. The cop came, and Dad sheepishly explained it was only his two-year-old daughter and not a robber. It was probably the most exciting thing that happened in that little one-horse town named Wheatland, California.

Years later, we lived in another small town (Livingston), and Dad was promoted to Loan Arranger for the B of A. They built a new bank, and our family and friends went down to help Dad move the stuff from the old bank to the new bank a couple of blocks down the street. It was a weekend, and Mom brought lunch down for us. While we were sitting around eating and drinking our sodas, someone said, "I wonder if that old vault alarm even works anymore." My dad walked over, put his hand on it, and was rewarded with an alarm that brought the cops. This time there were two.

# WHERE WILL IT LEAD?

IN THE BOOK *Fahrenheit 451*, they burned all the books, and I thought that would never happen. Then Madeline Murray O'Hare succeeded in banning Bible reading and prayer in schools. Before you know it, someone is going to suggest banning Dr. Suess, and I'm going to raise a ruckus.

MY HUSBAND SAYS THE pandemic restrictions are part of a conspiracy to control us. I'm okay with masks and staying away from large groups of people for a couple of years, but for those people who make their living from events with large numbers of people, I fear for them. Sports, concerts, eateries, movies, theaters, etc. I'm getting tired of my own cooking, even if Hello Fresh delivers all the ingredients. Oh, sure, we can order pizza, tacos, or Chinese take-out, but I want to sit down inside and get waited on, have water spilled in my lap, use a straw I have to ask for, and order from a menu I can touch.

# ESSENTIAL
# WORKERS

ESSENTIAL WORKERS DON'T have to worry about their income, but they have to worry about the new protocols on their jobs. Getting masked up and sprayed down. My son has to take a CoVid19 test every week and have his temperature taken each morning as he enters his work place. Many people who work in the medical field are exposed to CoVid19 all day, and when they come home to their families have to strip down at the door, shower, and in many cases, sleep in a separate room or the garage. My husband doesn't have CoVid19, but he snores so loudly, sleeping in another room would be a pleasure.

AFTER BEING A TEACHER most of my life, the ones I feel sorriest for are the teachers, especially if they have a bunch of their own kids at home. They have to plan lessons at home, learn the online technology, teach over Zoom or online while trying to help their own children who are also online taking classes and needing a parent's help. And then correct all the assignments that get sent to them from the students. It has got to be crazy in those households. How do they even have enough computers in the house for everyone? One teacher told me, while she was teaching a class on Zoom, some of the kids were jumping on their beds, going to the kitchen for snacks, and some disappeared off the screen altogether. The teacher is powerless to reach out and gently coax them back.

A great teacher I trained twenty-five years ago called to tell me he retired because he simply couldn't teach under those circumstances and restrictions. I can't imagine teaching without being able to pat a kid on the shoulder when he does well or hug a kid who needs a hug when he's hurting.

When computers were first introduced to schools, I wrote a letter to the school board and told them I didn't want one in my classroom. I was sure they were a passing fad and would come and go in a flurry. No sense wasting money on them. Now look at us. Everyone has a computer, if not at home then in their pocket or on their wrist.

I don't care how technologically dependent we become, teachers will always be essential workers.

I was listening to the radio in my car the other day while parked in the driveway pretending I had someplace to go. I heard a guy on the radio interviewing people regarding their feelings about the CoVid19 pandemic. One woman said it was a blessing. She bought herself a bike, lost fifty pounds, and was the healthiest she'd ever been. A tattoo artist called in and insisted that his business was essential because tattoos were good for people's mental health. I'm glad I wasn't driving; I would have driven into the ditch.

Thank goodness, Santa and his reindeers have been deemed essential.

# PHONE SOLICITORS

PHONE CALLS FROM SOLICITORS become my best entertainment. CoVid19 hasn't slowed them down a bit. At least they're consistent. There are three of them that haven't missed a day for three years. "Your Google listing hasn't been updated. Push 1 . . ." I'm not pushing anything except the cancel button, followed by the block button. Somehow they call on a different number every day.

Another one calls each day and says, "Medicare wants to send you a brace for your back pain for free." I don't have back pain (just a pain in my arse from repeated solicitors), and I do not require a back brace. I don't swear, but I swear, I want to. How many ways can one person say, "Don't call me again." I really should stay on the line and mess with them. I don't have anything else to do.

Almost every day I've won three days in a resort somewhere, a cruise, or a pile of money in a foreign country—all places I don't want to be right now.

# TRAVELING BY PLANE

WE FLEW TO MONTANA, and when we entered the plane, the cabin attendant handed us a little individual packet with a tiny-sanitized paper towel. Supposedly the whole plane has been sanitized, but I sanitized the tray, the handles, the back of the seat in front of me, and the guy next to me . . . "oops sorry, honey."

When it was time for a snack, the attendant handed each of us a plastic bag with a tiny bottle of water, a packaged cookie, a napkin, and some chips in their own bag. Someone had to put the bottle of water, the package of cookies, the chips, and the napkin in the plastic bag to hand to us. As a result, each bag of goodies actually got handled five or six times. Doesn't that seem counterproductive when we are trying not to spread germs?

# WHAT I LEARNED IN 2020

WHAT AM I MISSING? The bills still come, the sales catalogs still come, the solicitors still call, the newspaper still comes full of bad news.

WHAT AM I GLAD I'M missing? Expectations. Don't want to go to an event? "Sorry, CoVid19." Don't want to have a houseful of company for holidays? "Sorry, CoVid19." Don't want to babysit your neighbor's kids? "Sorry, CoVid19." We used to joke about playing the "C" card when my grandson and I had cancer, but now we have a new "C" card to play when we need an excuse to avoid participating in anything. And it works like a charm.

WHAT HAVE I LEARNED? I learned there are some people so stupid, they will rebel against the government, the virus, wearing masks, staying home, and shutting up. They think mouthing off, carrying signs, tearing up property, and hurting other people will somehow bring an end to the pandemic. They are what is called the "super spreaders." There's a good chance they are spreading the virus, as well as bad vibes and more discontent.

OUR LEADERS TELL US, "We're all in this together" No, we're not; we're all in this apart. While we are sequestered in our homes because there isn't a restaurant open for inside dining, our governor is dining in luxury with friends and family unmasked inside an upscale eatery. That's California for you.

# CONCLUSION

THERE ARE PROBABLY some hermit-type reclusive people who think this lockdown is just fine. I don't happen to be one of those people. I like people. I like to touch them, talk to them, share ideas with them, shake hands with them, eat with them, listen to them, and hug them. I don't like washing my hands every time I walk in the house or eating with my mouth closed. I like to slop things around the kitchen, lick my fingers, and talk with my mouth full. I don't like living by other people's rules, but I can do it if I have to.

In 1918 there was a huge pandemic, but when you look at the dates, you see 1917, 1918, and 1919. People were actually fined $25 if they stepped out in public without a mask. That amount to a lot of money in 1918. It's scary to think that this thing could last three years, but we can do it. I'll be eighty then, and I'm hoping this will be a distant memory and we'll be moving on to new challenges. In 2020 I wrote four books to various stages of completion. My goal is to have all four published by the end of 2021. To achieve that goal, I'll have to keep my nose to the grindstone and learn how to self-publish from online tutorials. If you're reading this, you'll know I'm making progress.

***PANDEMIC POEM*** by Karen Robertson
(Written and performed for the Zoom Poetry meeting of the Diamond Valley Writer's Guild in October 2020.)

"IT HAS BEEN THE WORST of times
　　and the best of times"

AFTER 30 YEARS IN ONE house
　　It's time we must deep clean
　　Some people do it regularly
　　I had to be quarantined.

DRAWERS, CLOSETS, AND patio
　　I have cleaned them all
　　Boxes I've transported
　　Goodwill, to them I haul.

OILED WOOD AND SWEPT cobwebs
　　Even dusted the top of the fans
　　Threw away old office supplies
　　And dried out rubber bands.

I'M NOT GOOD AT GARDENING,
　　but I enjoy pruning trees
　　Planting flowers, I detest
　　Frankly, so do my knees.

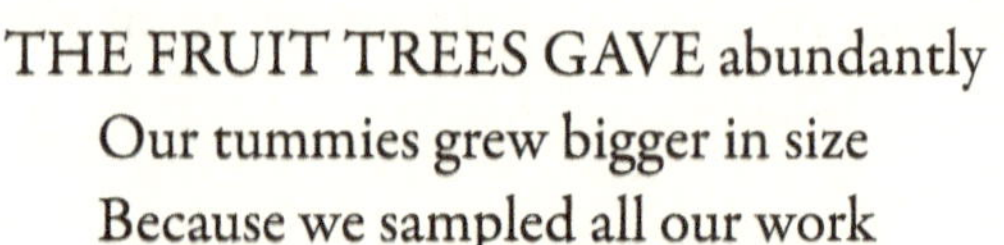

THE FRUIT TREES GAVE abundantly
    Our tummies grew bigger in size
    Because we sampled all our work
    We made some twenty-nine pies.

HELLO FRESH DELIVERED our food
    Meals for three days a week
    With a freezer full of pies and wild game
    The scales have begun to creak.

IF WE EVER NEEDED SOMETHING
    Our daughter-in-law would caper
    She wouldn't take any money
    So we paid her in toilet paper.

WE STAYED AWAY FROM all our friends
    We truly did our best
    A friend exposed us to CoVid19
    We were negative to the test.

THANKFUL FOR THE OUTCOME
    We hunkered down anew
    To make sure the test was right
    And we safely had come through.

SILVER SNEAKERS OFFERS classes
 For senior citizens like me
 Yoga, lifting and Pilates.
 I enjoyed some of all three.

MY DAUGHTER-IN-LAW invited me
 To take a class on line
 Tribal belly dancing it was called
 I pulled the curtains and the blinds.

I NEED A HAIRCUT AND a pedicure
 But I resist those public meets
 My hair looks like a Raggedy Ann
 My toenails are cutting the sheets.

I DON'T KNOW WHAT I would have done
 Without YouTube, Facebook, and Zoom
 Friends, family, and associates
 Were all right here in my room.

MY DAUGHTER HAD A STROKE last year
 Now we video chat each week
 It works as her speech therapy
 She can walk, she can drive, she can speak!

MY COMPUTER HAS BECOME my friend

For writing and communication
She's been ever faithful
During this incarceration.

BANANAGRAMS IS OUR competition
 We play each night after dinner
 We keep a running score on paper
 And right now, I'm the winner.

WE JUST ADDED CORNHOLE
 A game we play on the grass
 Barry beats me every time
 He can be such an . . . obnoxious winner.

WALKING KEEPS ME SANE each day
 As I walk miles and miles
 I pass people on the trails
 But I can't see their smiles.

SOME WEAR MASKS OR cover their face
 But nobody looks me in the eye
 We have lost so much in this country
 How long will we comply?

THIS WHOLE PANDEMIC thing
 Is crazy, if you ask me

But i think I've made the most of it
In a clean house that pleases me.

IT IS MY FAITH THAT keeps me strong
 No joy can compare
 With meeting God each morning
 When I talk with him in prayer.

AMEN

# SHOULD THIS BE THE END? NOT QUITE.

WHAT KIND OF TEACHER would I be without a vocabulary list?

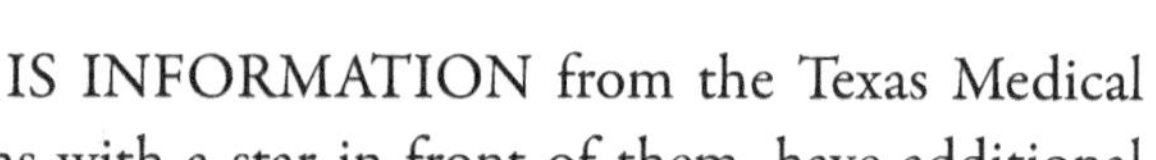

VOCABULARY LIST

WHAT FOLLOWS IS INFORMATION from the Texas Medical Center. The definitions with a star in front of them, have additional information I thought you might need to know.

ACUTE RESPIRATORY STRESS syndrome ARDS: A condition in which fluid builds up in the air sacs of the lungs. The fluid prohibits the lungs from getting enough air, leading to a deprivation of oxygen in the bloodstream. The condition is often fatal.

*ANTI-BODIES: ANTIBODIES are proteins produced by your immune system in response to an infection. (My cousin, her husband, and both daughters contracted CoVid19, got over it, and were tested for antibodies. When it was discovered they had the coveted antibodies, they were paid $400 each for donating blood. A week later the same cousin's husband went in to sell his anti-bodies, and they had changed the rules. He will get paid $700, but only after he gives blood seven times. The early bird gets the worm.)

*ASYMPTOMATIC: PRESENTING no symptoms of disease. Absence of fever, dry cough, sore throat, shortness of breath and body aches, among other less common symptoms. Being asymptomatic is one of the biggest problems because these are the people who can be super-spreaders without knowing it. (They are often the ones who opt not to wear masks because they are cocksure that they are home free.)

*CASE FATALITY RATE: the ration of deaths from CoVid19 compared to the total number of individuals diagnosed with the disease. (Statistics can be skewed and spewed in all different ways.)

*CLINICAL TRIAL: RESEARCH experiments on human participants designed to answer questions about new treatments, and safety and efficacy of a potential vaccine. (Otherwise known as guinea pigs on trial in a clinic.)

*COMMUNITY SPREAD: THE spread of a contagious disease in a geographic area in which there is no knowledge of how someone contracted the disease. No known contact can be traced to other infected individuals. (This is a mystery. Makes you wonder who is wandering outside the group for a little hanky-panky. Nobody is telling.)

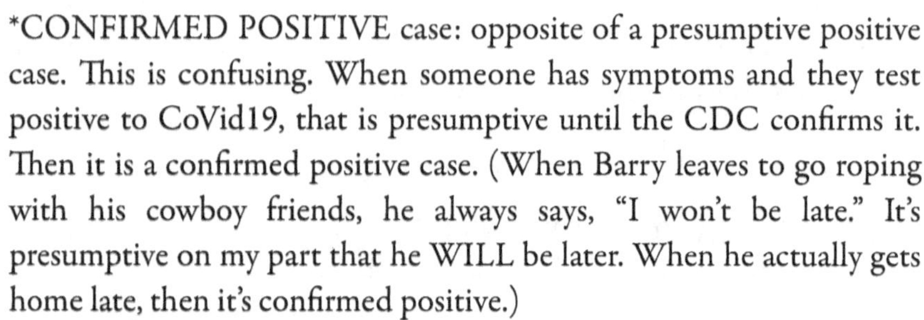

*CONFIRMED POSITIVE case: opposite of a presumptive positive case. This is confusing. When someone has symptoms and they test positive to CoVid19, that is presumptive until the CDC confirms it. Then it is a confirmed positive case. (When Barry leaves to go roping with his cowboy friends, he always says, "I won't be late." It's presumptive on my part that he WILL be later. When he actually gets home late, then it's confirmed positive.)

*CONTACT TRACING: IDENTIFYING and monitoring people who may have come into contact with an infectious person. Usually involves quarantine. (Medical people must feel like Sherlock Holmes when they are questioning people to try to trace where they contacted someone with CoVid19.)

*CONTACTLESS DELIVERY: leaving purchase items at the entryway of a home rather than handing it directly to a person. (Hello Fresh is contactless delivery. They put the box of food in the garage. If we aren't home, they put it on the ground by the gate. Lots of stores have advertised contactless delivery so nobody touches anyone. Also, outside pick-up is advertised by many businesses, where you communicate through cellphone and stay in the car.)

*CONTAINMENT AREA: A geographical zone with limited access in or out in an effort to contain an outbreak. (Communes, cults, senior facilities, and Area 51.)

*CORONAVIRUS: A FAMILY of viruses that include SARS (Severe acute respiratory syndrome) and MERS (Middle East Respiratory Syndrome) as well as other respiratory illnesses. Another coronavirus, also known as CoV, is typically spread between animals and humans—an event known as zoonotic transfer—and they are named for the term "corona," Latin for crown, which refers to the shape of the virus when observed microscopically. (If that's true, should dogs and cats be wearing masks?)

*COVID19 STANDS FOR novel coronavirus disease 2019, which refers to the year of its initial detection. CoVid19 is the illness related to the current pandemic; the illness is caused by the virus SARS-Cov2 (severe acute respiratory syndrome coronavirus 2). (No matter what you call it, CoVid19 has really made a mess of things.)

*EPIDEMIC: A WIDESPREAD occurrence of an infectious disease in a community or geographic area. (When my mom came home from the hospital after giving birth to my little sister, I started an epidemic of chicken pox in our household. Mom got chicken pox and so did my infant sister, Linda. I understand nursing my little sister was very painful for my mother, but it was not a conspiracy to protest the loss of my title as "only child.")

*EPIDEMIC CURVE: A GRAPH or chart depicting the progression of an outbreak in a particular population. (Or a woman who outgrows a new pair of pants every year.)

*EPIDEMIOLOGY: A BRANCH of medicine which deals largely with public health, including the incidence, distribution, analysis, and control of diseases. (They probably haven't had this much media coverage since the N1H1 Swine flu. Even then, nobody fessed up to kissing pigs.)

*ESSENTIAL BUSINESSES: groceries, pharmacies, waste collection, health care providers, gas stations, banks, transportation, and agriculture services. (First responders and teachers should have made the list. And what about postal workers, delivery workers, truck drivers, and so many more. I think my hairdresser and pedicurist should have been included.)

*FLATTENING THE CURVE: an attempt to create a more gradual uptick of cases. (I thought flattening the curve had something to do with sit-ups and jumping jacks. Or is it one of those girdles I see on Facebook you can tuck all your fat into and look svelte?)

*FOREHEAD THERMOMETER: (There's a forehead thermometer at the gym. The other day it showed my temperature at 91 degrees. If a temperature of 100 degrees means you're sick, and 98.6 is normal, I must be getting *weller* and *weller*.)

*HERD IMMUNITY: ALSO known as community immunity, this is the reduction of risk or infection within a population, often because of previous exposure or vaccinations.

(I thought that was a bunch of cows that escaped mad-cow disease.)

*HYDROXYCHLOROQUINE: an oral drug used to treat malaria, rheumatoid arthritis, and lupus. (Its use in CoVin19 is questionable and unproven, but they'll try anything once.)

IMMUNE SURVEILLANCE: the process of monitoring the immune systems activities, which may include the detection and destruction of foreign substances, cells, or tissues.

*IMMUNOSUPPRESSED: AN individual who experiences reduced efficacy of the immune system as a result of health conditions not related to CoVid19 disease. People who are immunosuppressed are at greater risk for hospitalization and severe sickness from the SARS-CoV-2 virus. (No kidding, this includes those who have underlying conditions like diabetes, obesity, heart issues, cancer, emphysema, and decrepitness.)

*INCUBATION PERIOD: the time between when an individual is first exposed to the virus and the appearance of symptoms. (Or the time it takes to hatch an egg.)

*INDEX CASE: THE FIRST documented case of an infectious disease. (Not a distinction that warrants a reward of any kind.)

*INDEX PATIENT: THE first person infected with a disease in an epidemic, interchangeable with the term "patient zero." (Whoop dee doo! Wouldn't you love to have this title?)

*INTENSIVIST: A PHYSICIAN who specializes in treating patients who are in intensive care or in intensive care units. (That's intense!)

*LOCK DOWN: AN EMERGENCY measure in which individuals are restricted to certain areas in an attempt to control exposure or transmission of disease. (Recommendation-Stay home!)

*NATIONAL EMERGENCY: a state of emergency resulting from the global threat of the pandemic. March 13, 2020, President Trump issued a national emergency concerning the CoVid19 outbreak. (From there on, there was the Blame Game, mass chaos and total confusion. No matter what a person died from it was deemed CoVid19. Motorcycle accident . . . CoVid19. Fell off a roof . . . CoVid19. Rattlesnake bite . . . CoVid19.)

*PANDEMIC: A WORLDWIDE spread of an infectious diseases, with larger reach than an epidemic. Until CoVid19, the last pandemic was the H1N1 influenza outbreak in 2009. (We got past that; let's get past this!)

*PERSON-TO-PERSON TRANSMISSION: coughing, sneezing, (picking your nose after shopping, rubbing your eyes, kissing an infected person, or having an infected person stick his finger in your eye.)

*PHYSICAL DISTANCING: the practice of maintaining greater space between oneself and others and /or avoiding direct contact with other people. (Six feet is suggested and there are paper feet stuck on the floor in case you don't know how to estimate six feet.)

*PPE: PERSONAL PROTECTIVE equipment, specialized clothing and equipment used as a safeguard against health hazards. Nose, eyes, hands, feet, and mouth are covered. (I consider my go-kart racing helmet my PPE, but it wouldn't protect me from the virus.)

*PRE-SYMPTOMATIC: THIS is before you experience any symptoms. (Pre means before. My doctor says I'm pre-diabetic. Aren't we all pre-diabetic if we aren't diabetic yet? Isn't everybody pre-symptomatic if they haven't had symptoms yet?)

*PRESUMPTIVE POSITIVE case: an individual who has tested positive for CoVid by local public health lab, but whose results are awaiting confirmation from the CDC. (If you think you have CoVid, you test positive for CoVid, and you are sick as a dog with CoVid, it's only presumptive positive until the CDC declares it confirmed positive.)

*PUI: PERSON UNDER INVESTIGATION . . . suspected of potentially having CoVid. (This may come from a command center manned by Big Brother watching to see who sneezes or coughs.)

*REMDESIVIR: AN INVESTIGATIONAL antiviral drug that is administered intravenously and inhibits viral replication. It is a promising drug for the treatment of CoVid19 disease and was first developed to treat Ebola. (Maybe)

RESPIRATOR: A DEVICE designed to protect individuals from inhaling something hazardous in the air, in this case, particulates that may be contaminated with the SARS-COV 2 virus.

*SARS-COV2: THE VIRUS fully defined as "severe acute respiratory syndrome coronavirus 2" causes the disease CoVid19. (Some fool in a science lab was trying to be creative. That's what happens when the teacher leaves the room.)

*SCREENING: THE ACT of verifying symptoms and potential exposure before testing for the virus. (Questions like: Can you taste or smell? Are you coughing or sneezing? Do you have a fever? Not too effective if you happen to be asymptomatic.)

*SELF-ISOLATION: THE act of separating oneself from others. (Hermitism. Some people prefer this to the traditional Thanksgiving gathering.)

*SELF-QUARANTINE: THE act of refraining from any contact with other individuals for a period of time—in the case of CoVid19, two weeks—to observe whether any symptoms of the disease will arise after potential exposure. (Some people self-quarantine from their relatives for an unlimited amount of time to see if better relations arise.)

*SHELTER-IN-PLACE: TYPICALLY issued by local government, a shelter-in-place asks residents to remain at home and only leave to perform duties deemed essential in an effort to slow transmission of the exposure to the virus. (I have no problem staying at home, but Barry has cattle that need herding, a golf ball that needs chasing, and Jalapeno Frito's waiting at the store for him to purchase them.)

*SOCIAL DISTANCING: the act of remaining physically apart in an effort to stem transmission of CoVid19. Social distancing can include a move to remote work, the cancellation of events, and remaining at least six feet away from other individuals. (No hugging, rubbing up against people or tackling. You shouldn't spit on others either.)

*SPANISH FLU: ALSO KNOWN as the 1918 influenza pandemic. This was the most severe pandemic in recent history, according to the Centers of Disease Control and Prevention (CDC), with an estimated 500 million infections and 50 million deaths worldwide. It was caused by an H1N1 virus with genes of an avian origin. (What bird is Spanish? Or was it the bird fly? Or the bird flew?)

*SUPER-SPREADER: A HIGHLY contagious individual who can spread an infectious disease to a large number of uninfected people through a network of contacts. (Laughter is contagious, so Jerry Seinfeld could be considered a super-spreader.)

*SYMPTOMATIC: SHOWING symptoms of CoVid19, which can include fever, dry cough, shortness of breath, loss of taste and smell, and body aches. Health officials believe the risk of transmitting the virus is highest when an individual is symptomatic. (Kind of like comedy. When the comic is on stage saying funny stuff, the risk of spreading laughter is at its highest.)

*VACCINE: A BIOLOGICAL preparation of organisms that provides immunity to a particular infectious disease. (Currently, there two vaccines for CoVid19. Say what you will about vaccines, but when my mom was a kid, she got Scarlet Fever and Smallpox, my X-husband had polio, and I had the measles several times, as well as Chicken Pox, and best of all, mumps for my fifteenth birthday on Christmas Day. All of those diseases are seldom heard of, wiped out by vaccines. Someday we'll look back on 2020 and say, "Thank you, Lord, for giving our scientists the knowledge they needed to make a vaccine that wiped out CoVid19."

I recently got my second shingles and annual flu vaccines. My arms were sore for several days, but I'm better off not getting those diseases at my age. I wish they had a vaccine against fat.)

*VENTILATOR: A MACHINE designed to move air in and out of the lungs for a patient who is physically unable to breathe or who is not breathing well. Because CoVid19 can cause severe lower respiratory infection, ventilators are a critical machine for patients with severe disease. (A ventilator kept my daughter alive for two weeks while she was in a medically induced coma after a massive stroke. Now she's walking two miles a day, beating me at word games, and driving her new car. Thank you God for ventilators.)

*WFH: AN ABBREVIATION for "working from home." (Or "what freaky hours.")

PANDEMICS OF THE PAST

Past pandemics that have been recorded were in 1918, 1957-8, 1968, 2009 and 2020.

Interesting fact I discovered: since 1918 the gaps between pandemics has been approximately, forty, ten, forty, and ten years. Hopefully, that means it will be another forty years before the next pandemic, and I won't be around to worry about it. A happy thought to end on.

THE END

# ACKNOWLEDGEMENTS

THANK YOU TO MY FRIEND Penny Beaulieu who offered stellar ideas, most of which I ignored, Kathi Macias who edited the book and made it readable, the person who challenged me to write this book whose name I can't remember, and Michele Van Dusen who is a fellow comic, always an encourager and begged to be mentioned.

# ABOUT THE
# AUTHOR

KAREN ROBERTSON LIVES in Wildomar, California with her husband Barry. She has retired from education, real estate, coaching, clowning and comedy. Her writing always includes humor and how God is working in her life or the life of her characters. Most recently she has written two novels, *The Turnaround* and *Turnaround at Sea* (Available March 2021).

Contact her for speaking engagements or to tell her how you enjoyed her writing: <u>kanwrite@SayItWithHumor.com</u> You will also find some of her comedy videos[1] here. Check out her TEDx speech on the power of humor titled *Livin' Life Laughing*[2].

---

1.    http://www.sayitwithhumor.com/

2.    *https://www.youtube.com/watch?v=pc5bGXUQyT0*

# Don't miss out!

Visit the website below and you can sign up to receive emails whenever KAREN ROBERTSON publishes a new book. There's no charge and no obligation.

https://books2read.com/r/B-A-PCHM-KZNLB

BOOKS 2 READ

Connecting independent readers to independent writers.

Did you love *Pandemic Pandemonium*? Then you should read *More for Les*[3] by KAREN ROBERTSON!

So, there I was, standing shoulder-to-shoulder with Mark Wahlberg. Most women would say, "A dream come true," but in my case, it was a prayer answered. He is adorable, but I'm over seventy, and I was on a mission.

Sure, I've dreamed of being a movie star, but on that day my title was "unpaid extra" in a movie I would never go to the theater to see . . . R-rated . . . but I had a reason for being there and only God could have orchestrated it. It was October 2014. Here's the story of how I appeared in the ComiCon scene with Mark Wahlberg in Ted 2. I'll start from the beginning.

---

3. https://books2read.com/u/3R8xAB

4. https://books2read.com/u/3R8xAB

In 2003, right after his fourth birthday, my grandson, Les Paul Fountain was diagnosed with medullablastoma, otherwise known as fast-growing pediatric brain cancer. As a result of the tumor, surgery, radiation, and chemotherapy, he would never be a "typical" kid again. He's Special.

This is my story about Les and me. I know I'm not your average grandparent. When Les was diagnosed, I was retired. I'd been a teacher, administrator, success coach, clown, real estate salesperson, freelance writer, tour guide, and motivational speaker. I wanted to use all those skills to help Les. . . and I lived close andI had time.

My motivation for telling this story is to encourage others whose lives are intertwined with a special person who needs your help. You might be a teacher, a doctor, a parent, a relative or a friend; this is for you.

www.ingramcontent.com/pod-product-compliance
Lightning Source LLC
Chambersburg PA
CBHW021020160726
47994CB00006B/2596